Chrissy`s Mandalas

I hope you enjoy coloring these images as much as I did making them.

Happy Coloring!

Each coloring page is printed on a separate sheet to avoid bleed through.

Christine Hardy
Copyright 2016

Copyright 2016

Christine Hardy

Copyright 2016

Christine Hardy

Copyright 2016

Christine Hardy

Copyright 2016

Copyright 2016

Christine Hardy

Copyright 2016

Christine Hardy

Copyright 2016

Christine Hardy

Copyright 2016

Christine Hardy

Copyright 2016

Christine Hardy

Copyright 2016

Christine Hardy

Copyright 2016

Christine Hardy

Copyright 2016

Copyright 2016

Christine Hardy

Copyright 2016

Christine Hardy

Copyright 2016

Christine Hardy

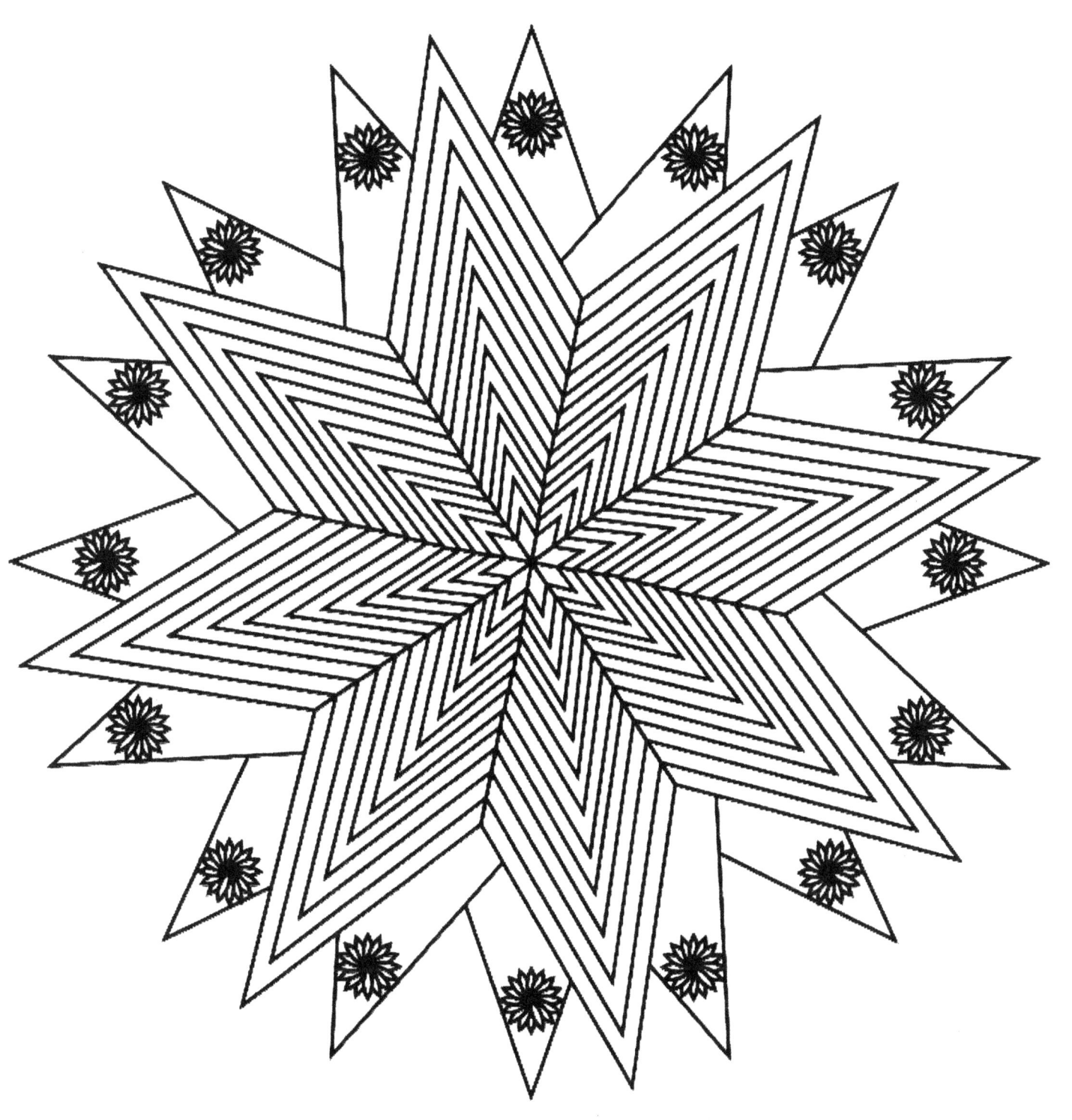

Copyright 2016

Christine Hardy

Copyright 2016

Christine Hardy

Copyright 2016

Christine Hardy

Copyright 2016

Christine Hardy

Copyright 2016

Christine Hardy

Copyright 2016

Christine Hardy

Copyright 2016

Christine Hardy

Copyright 2016

Christine Hardy

Copyright 2016

Christine Hardy

Copyright 2016

Christine Hardy

Copyright 2016

Christine Hardy

Christine Hardy

Copyright 2016

Christine Hardy

Copyright 2016

Christine Hardy

Copyright 2016

Christine Hardy

Included with this coloring book are 30 smaller images that you can use to test your color combinations

All images are identical to the images in this Coloring Book!

The smaller images in this Coloring Book are for your personal use only.
You cannot reproduce,sell,give away freely or modify these images in any way.

CopyRight 2016   Christine Hardy

Copyright 2016 Christine Hardy

Copyright 2016 Christine Hardy

Copyright 2016   Christine Hardy

www.ingramcontent.com/pod-product-compliance
Lightning Source LLC
Chambersburg PA
CBHW081404280526
45788CB00009B/2979